ECONOMICS

Eduard Altarriba

Button
BOOKS

**Blessed are the young,
for they shall inherit the national debt.**

Herbert Hoover (President of the United States, 1929–1933)

Contents

INTRODUCTION

The ECONOMY is everywhere: when you buy bread, when a container of goods arrives in port, when a tin of cookies leaves the factory, when someone buys shares in a company, when you take money out of an ATM, when a war breaks out, when you pay taxes, when you go on vacation . . .

ECONOMISTS are people who try to understand and explain how this complex system works. But even they don't agree on how to make sense of the economy and what the ideal economic system should be.

WHAT IS ECONOMICS?

Economics is the social science that studies how resources (which are scarce and limited) are used to meet people's needs.

Imagine a village of shepherds whose only product is goats. The goats' milk is used to make cheese.

One shepherd has five goats. He is the richest man in the village and can make the most cheese.

Another shepherd has two goats, while the poorest only has one goat and can barely make enough cheese to eat.

The village's wealth is eight goats (and the cheese they make), but it is not shared out equally.

SURPLUS

Besides raising goats and making cheese, many other jobs need to be done in the village so that everything runs properly: weaving, cooking, gathering firewood, building fences, looking after children . . .

The richest shepherd has more cheese than he and his family can eat. He has a SURPLUS. He can exchange the cheese he doesn't need for wheat from the lord of the neighboring village. His wife makes bread with this wheat, which she EXCHANGES with the other shepherds for more cheese.

Perhaps one day in that little village there will be a lord with lots of goats, and shepherds working for him. And soldiers who will defend the village. And a blacksmith who will forge tools and weapons, and a carpenter, and a merchant, and a priest . . .

The village's needs will have permanently changed and be more complex, and the surplus will be used to meet these needs (such as paying taxes, maintaining the army, trading, and making offerings to the gods).

money

You know what this is. When you go to buy bread or a book, you pay a certain amount of coins or banknotes in the store and, in return, they give you the bread or the book. But where does the money come from? Who makes it, and how?

Let's go back a bit. In our village, the rich shepherd exchanged cheese for wheat. In the same way, cheese can be exchanged for fish, fish for apples, or apples for tools.

Exchanging things to do business is called BARTER.

But what happens if someone has fish and needs firewood, and another person has firewood but doesn't need fish and instead needs a new ax?

And how do we work out how much firewood a fish is worth, or how many fish an ax is worth?

Also, some goods, like fish, go bad very quickly and can't be stored for long.

That's why societies started looking for objects that could be offered in exchange instead of goods. For someone to accept an object instead of goods, they would have to be happy that they could then offer that object to someone else in exchange for other goods. That meant the object should be easy to carry, hard-wearing (so you knew you could use it in the future), and also be of value to other people (so you knew someone else would offer goods in exchange for it). Such objects are known as CURRENCIES.

COINS

Throughout history, many things have been used as CURRENCY: shells in Africa, salt in ancient Rome, rice in China, cocoa beans in the Americas.

Some of the biggest "coins" in the world are stones with holes in them that were used on the Yap Islands in Micronesia. They weighed up to five tons!

In some places, such as Mesopotamia and China, people started using metal ingots such as bronze or iron. But the main metals used as money were gold and silver. These are quite rare materials and they don't rust.

The problem with metal ingots is they are heavy and hard to transport. So people began to divide them into smaller, often round, pieces known as coins.

Each coin had its own value depending on the material it was made of and its weight.

MINTING a coin means stamping the symbol of the authority that has made it, such as a king or queen, city, or country.

This man is minting coins by stamping a drawing on them.

Blank gold coins

Minted coins

The first known coins were made near present-day Turkey 2,500 years ago.

Cities and kingdoms began minting their own coins in workshops called mints in order to standardize weights and values and prevent forgeries.

As there were so many different currencies, it was not always easy for merchants to change their prices from one type of currency to another. That is why specialist money changers appeared.

Gold and silver were very scarce, so they soon started to be mixed with cheaper metals. This lowered their value, but allowed more coins to be minted. Nowadays, coins are made from cheap metals.

Silver tetradrachm
from Athens
(454 to 404 BCE)

Gold dinar
from Damascus
(7th century CE)

Bronze coin
from the Tang dynasty
(7th to 10th century)

Silver dollar
from the USA
(1794)

TRADE

The use of coins made it easier for wealth to be transported from one place to another, even on long journeys by land or sea.

> I have 5 coins to be able to trade.

> I buy wheat from this Iberian for 3 coins.

> I travel.

> I sell the wheat to this Numidian for 5 coins, but I buy her fabrics and pay her 6 coins.

> Then I go home and sell the fabrics for 10 coins.

Buying and selling goods is called TRADE.

The people who buy things at one price and sell them at a higher price are called TRADERS.

The SILK ROAD was one of the most important TRADE ROUTES in history. It wasn't just one road: it was a network of different routes that connected Europe to Asia via the Arab world.

Caravans went from city to city and goods were bought and sold many times before they reached their final destination. Ideas, knowledge, and diseases were also transported along the Silk Road.

Money was also used to pay for SERVICES, such as mercenaries who fought in exchange for a salary. These days, most people receive a SALARY in exchange for the work they do.

THE FIRST BANKS

Some MONEY CHANGERS built up enough wealth to be able to lend money to other people, from traders who needed money to do business, to kings and princes who needed it to finance their wars. That's how the first bankers appeared.

> I need a thousand coins to hire a merchant ship.

Transporting a large quantity of coins is difficult because it weighs a lot and it might attract the attention of thieves and bandits.

**So in some places they started using bills of exchange instead.
In China, they were doing this over a thousand years ago.**

Imagine there's a storekeeper who buys a shipment of tea from a trader. The storekeeper hasn't yet had time to sell the tea and has no money to pay the trader, so instead he signs a piece of paper that says how much money he owes and when he will pay it. The trader can use this bill of exchange to buy goods from another trader, as if it were "paper money."

BANKNOTES

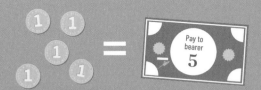

Banknotes are used in the same way as coins, but they are pieces of paper with no physical value. Each banknote is equivalent to a certain amount of wealth, whether it is coins, gold, or other goods. To stop banks printing mountains of them, it was decided to link the value of each banknote to a real value: <u>the gold standard</u> (see page 12). This meant banknotes and coins could only be issued on the basis of a country's gold reserves.

The CENTRAL BANK in each country is responsible for printing banknotes and minting coins in its currency.

In Europe, banknotes were rare until the 17th century, when people who deposited coins in banks started to be given a deposit slip, a piece of paper that stated the amount deposited.

This piece of paper could be used as currency and passed from hand to hand because, unlike bills of exchange, it didn't have a name or date on it: anyone who had one could go to the bank and exchange it for coins.

At first, each bank had its own banknotes. Soon, though, governments began to produce banknotes for each country that could be used in all the banks.

—THE GOLD STANDARD—

*Until the mid-20th century, the amount of money available in cash in a country was linked to its gold reserves: **each banknote corresponded to a small part of the gold that the state had in storage**, and (in theory) everyone could go to the **central bank** and ask to exchange their banknotes for gold.*

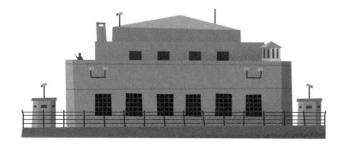

Fort Knox is the place where the USA keeps most of its gold reserves. It is one of the most heavily protected places in the world.

But there is only a limited amount of gold in the world, and this made it more difficult for countries to achieve economic growth.

So, in the mid-20th century, politicians and economists decided to move away from the gold standard and use something else as a guide: the currency of the economy that was the most powerful in the world (at that time), and had the most gold—the US dollar.

—TRUST—

The coins we use these days are made from cheap metals and our banknotes are pieces of paper or plastic with no real value (and are not linked to gold reserves). So, why do we trust in their value? Why do we think that a $100 bill is worth a hundred dollars and a €10 note is worth ten euros?

We trust in this because we know there is a government, a central bank, and an economic, political, and legal system that guarantees its value. Money is a fiction and the whole of society believes it.

Banknotes have very complicated drawings to make them difficult to forge.

In principle, inside a country you can only use that country's coins and banknotes.

Only governments are allowed to issue stamps and official documents.

- PRINTING MONEY -

Each country's government, through its CENTRAL BANK, is responsible for printing money and trying to make sure the economy is stable.

We might think that we could solve poverty just by printing and distributing more banknotes.

But it's not that simple. As we have already explained, banknotes have no value in themselves, but are a reflection of a country's economy.

Printing more banknotes than are needed can lead to money losing value and cause INFLATION.

- INFLATION AND DEFLATION -

INFLATION is when the PRICE of things GOES UP continuously over a period of time.
DEFLATION is the exact opposite: a general FALL IN PRICES.

In 1921, $1 was worth 60 marks. → In 1922, $1 was worth 8,000 marks!

Other things can also cause inflation, such as the price of oil going up or there being a lot of demand for some products. If prices go up a lot, we call it hyperinflation.

During the First World War, Germany printed a lot of paper money (it issued lots more banknotes than it should have done based on how much gold it had).

Then, when Germany lost the war, it carried on issuing lots more paper money so that it could pay for the damage caused by the war. As a result, the mark (the German currency) suffered from terrible hyperinflation.

People watched as their savings lost value and prices carried on going up. A loaf of bread ended up costing 3 billion marks! People went back to exchanging things because money was basically worthless.

●●CURRENCIES●● ●

Every country has its own money. So if you go to the USA, you have to pay in American dollars, if you go to Japan you use yen, and in most countries in the European Union, you use euros.

But when you use money outside of its country (or union of countries), it's called a currency.

SOME OF THE MOST WIDELY TRADED CURRENCIES IN THE WORLD

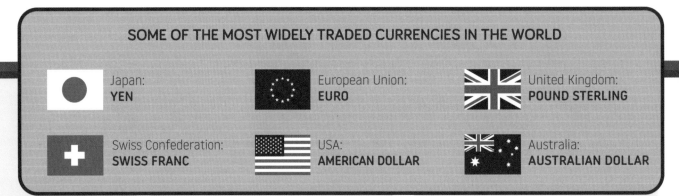

Japan:
YEN

European Union:
EURO

United Kingdom:
POUND STERLING

Swiss Confederation:
SWISS FRANC

USA:
AMERICAN DOLLAR

Australia:
AUSTRALIAN DOLLAR

Currencies can be exchanged, and this makes their price change in relation to other currencies.

For example, one day you can buy one dollar for one euro and a few weeks later you might need one and a half euros to buy one dollar.

Some currencies change value in relation to others very quickly, and others are more stable (their value doesn't change that much and changes more slowly).

These price variations between different currencies are very important, for example, for international trade, as they affect goods that are imported and exported and paid for in different currencies.

ELCOME TO USA

US DOLLAR EXCHANGE RATES	
Euro	0.91
British Pound	0.80
Indian Rupee	81.84
Australian Dollar	1.49
Swiss Franc	0.89
Japanese Yen	133.47
Chinese Yuan	6.87

You'll probably already have seen a bank card or someone buying something on the internet.

These days, we are seeing a real revolution in the way we use money: we are using fewer and fewer coins and banknotes to pay for things.

MR JOHN SMITH

MONEY IS INFORMATION

Increasingly, money and wealth go from one company to another and one country to another through computer networks. Now it's no longer banknotes or coins, but information that circulates, adding and subtracting money from bank accounts.

Mia works in a store and every month her salary is paid into her bank account.	She can check if she's been paid by going to her bank's website or app and checking her balance.	With the money she has in her account, she can buy things on the internet or pay by card in a store.

 # CRYPTOCURRENCY

Maybe you've heard people talking about cryptocurrencies such as Bitcoin or Ethereum. Some people say they are the future of money, but others are not so sure and think they are dangerous because they are not issued by central banks. There are lots of them, but they all use more or less the same system.

Governments and central banks don't have control over cryptocurrencies.	*Everybody can use them but there is no physical money: they only come in digital form.*	*They don't exist on just one computer: they use a technology called "blockchain" that shares information around the world.*	*There are a limited number of coins of each cryptocurrency, and one day, it won't be possible to make any more.*

CREATING MONEY

Lots of people have a BANK ACCOUNT.

When you have a bank account, you can see a list that tells you how much money has been paid in and what you have spent (your "transactions"), as well as how much money you have left (your "balance").

	TRANSACTIONS	BALANCE
Day 4	-$50	$100
Day 3	+$75	$150
Day 2	-$25	$75
Day 1	$100	$100

Mr Garcia has a $100 bill which he pays into his bank account. The bank keeps the $100 in a safe.

If you look at the bank, there's only one $100 bill, but Mr Garcia has $100 in his current account and Mia has $75 in her current account. In total, there are $175 in circulation.

But what if Mr Garcia wants his $100 bill back? The bank still has the $100 bill, but what if Mia also wants her $75 in banknotes?

LEGAL RESERVE

Banks use most of the money that is deposited to lend or invest. But in many countries they must keep a small amount in reserve. In Europe, banks must keep €1 out of every €100 deposited.

OUT OF NOTHING ①

Mia needs money to buy a gift, so she goes to the bank and asks them to lend her $75.

The bank has the $100 bill in its safe. They decide to lend Mia the money by transferring $75 to her bank account.

$100 + $75 = $175

And if Mia buys the gift in a store and the storekeeper deposits the $75 in the bank, and the bank lends it out again, there will be even more money in circulation.

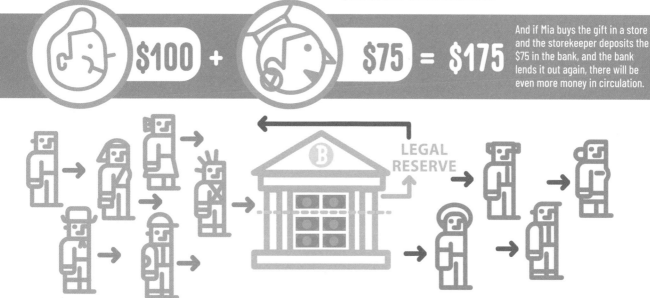

LEGAL RESERVE

But for this to work, the bank needs lots of people to be circulating money (putting money in and taking money out): thousands like Mr Garcia, who deposit money, and thousands like Mia, who withdraw money they have in their bank account.

But what would happen if everyone decided to take the money out at the same time? Well, the bank would have a problem (and so would the people who lent the money), as there would not be enough reserves. The bank would simply not be able to give people their money back in cash.

The government could step in to protect the banks (and the whole economic system) by telling people they're not allowed to withdraw their money.

CREATING MONEY

Banks lend money (to people, companies, countries, and other banks), but they don't do it because they are really nice people. They do it because it's the main part of their business.

When they lend money to someone like Mia, they do it under certain conditions: Mia will have to pay back all the money they lent her and a little bit more: THE INTEREST.

INTEREST

Interest is the extra percentage (%) that you pay on a sum of money after a certain time.

 BUT WHAT IS A PERCENTAGE?

When, for example, we talk about paying a percentage of 5%, it means that for every $100, we pay an extra $5.

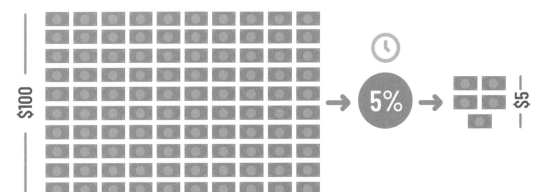

So if we have to pay back a loan of 5% on $100, we have to pay back $105.

OUT OF NOTHING ②

MR GARCIA PUTS HIS $100 IN THE BANK. IT WILL GIVE HIM 1% INTEREST PER YEAR.

MIA BORROWED $75, AND HAS TO PAY IT BACK ALONG WITH 5% INTEREST.

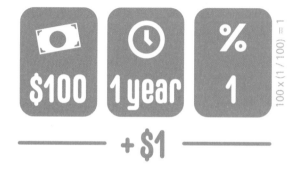

$100 \times (1/100) = 1$

+ $1

$75 \times (5/100) = 3.75$

+$3.75

This means that if he leaves the money in the bank for a year, when he takes it out, the bank will give him $101.

This means at the end of the year she has to pay back the money. As the bank lent her $75, she will have to pay back $78.75 in total.

$3.75 − $1 = **+$2.75** Overall money that the bank earns

For the bank it was worth lending part of the money deposited by Mr Garcia, because it paid out $1 in interest but earned $3.75, so it has ended up with $2.75 more than it started with.

INTEREST = a percentage (%) applied to an amount of money.
This can be money deposited in the bank or lent by the bank.

Earning $2.75 may not sound like much. But if Mr Garcia had deposited $1,000,000 and was paid 1% interest (so $10,000), and the bank lent a total $750,000 and was paid 5% interest (so $37,500), the bank would earn $27,500 simply from loaning out Mr Garcia's money!

THINGS WE CAN DO IN A BANK

USE THE ATM TO WITHDRAW CASH OR CHECK HOW MUCH MONEY YOU HAVE

HAVE A SAVINGS ACCOUNT

Unlike a checking account, a savings account is our "piggy bank." You can't use this money for a certain period of time, but in return the bank pays you higher interest.

PENSION PLANS are the money you save to use when you retire from work.

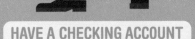

HAVE A CHECKING ACCOUNT

People usually keep their money in a checking or current account (it has different names in different countries). This is like our "safe" that we can use to make and receive payments.

EARNINGS: your salary is paid into your checking account.

DIRECT DEBITS: basic expenses such as rent or electricity bills are automatically paid out every month.

BANK CARDS

You can have a bank card linked to your checking account.

With a **DEBIT CARD** you can withdraw money from an ATM or use the money in your checking account to pay for things in stores or online.

With a **CREDIT CARD** you can do the same things, but using money the bank lends to you. Later, you will have to pay back this money with interest.

BORROW MONEY

When people or companies need money to invest or they have big expenses, they go to the bank to borrow money.

But the bank doesn't lend money to everyone, and if you can't repay the loan the bank may take what you were trying to buy.

PERSONAL LOANS are used to buy things such as a computer or a car. The money must be paid back with interest over a certain period of time.

MORTGAGES are very big loans that people usually ask for to buy a house. They are paid back with interest over many years. The house you buy also serves as security for payment.

SIGNING UP FOR PRODUCTS

The bank offers a number of services and products that you can invest your money in to make a profit (the money generated by interest).

INVESTMENT FUNDS collect money from lots of people in order to earn more money than each person could make alone.

INSURANCE is money you pay every month so that you will get paid if the thing you have insured is damaged (you can insure your house, your health, a car, and many other things).

Until recently, people used to go to the bank in their city or neighborhood to use the banking services. These days, you can still visit banks in most towns, but many people do their banking on the internet.

MARKETS

Markets are places where things are bought and sold.

When someone goes to the market for apples, for example, he or she is a *BUYER* who wants to buy the best apples at the lowest possible price.

The *SELLER* wants to sell their apples at the highest possible price.

However, when we're talking about economics, "the market" isn't like the ones in town. Instead, it's a way of referring to all the spaces (physical, virtual, or both) where all kinds of products and services are offered, bought, and sold.

So, there are markets like the art market (with its galleries, museums, collectors, and critics), the job market (with job supply and demand), and the stock market (see page 42).

PROFITS

By the time a product, such as a tin of cookies, reaches the market, there have been lots of different people and companies involved, and lots of production costs.

The companies involved in making, selling, and transporting the product all expect to make money.

In other words, they expect to have a PROFIT MARGIN.

THE FARMER

Sells each sack of wheat for $2
But it costs him $1 to produce each sack (he has to pay for costs such as machinery, labor, and fuel).

PROFITS: **$1 per sack**

THE INTERMEDIARY

Sells each sack of wheat for $4
She buys the wheat from farmers for $2 per sack and sells it to factories. It costs her an extra $1 per sack to manage warehouses and trucks.

PROFITS: **$1 per sack**

WHAT ARE THINGS WORTH?

Many things that are bought or sold have a use: you can use a fishing rod to fish, or grain to grow wheat. They have a use value, and the price someone will pay for them will depend on how useful they think they will be.

But use value can change in different circumstances. For example, on an island surrounded by water you'd find a fishing rod very useful. However, it wouldn't be very useful to you in the middle of a desert with no water for hundreds of miles.

We don't only think something is valuable because of how useful it is. Whether we like or dislike it will also change its value to us. We may buy flowers to decorate our home because they look pretty, or we may spend lots of money on our favorite football team's jersey while we wouldn't accept a rival team's jersey even if it was free.

THE FACTORY

Sells each tin for $8
It costs $6 to produce each tin of cookies ($4 for each sack of wheat, plus $2 for costs such as rent, wages, and electricity).
PROFITS: **$2 per tin**

THE STORE

Sells each tin for $12
It costs the store $10 to sell each tin of cookies ($8 paid to the factory, plus $2 for rent, taxes, electricity, and so on).
PROFITS: **$2 per tin**

To find out a product's profit margin you need to subtract the money it cost you to buy or make it from the price you sold it for.

If you end up with less than the production cost, you have lost money. If you end up with more, you have made money. However, if you charge too much, people might decide to buy the product from someone else.

So, how are prices decided?

The economic value or price of a product or service is set when it is put on the market.

HOW MARKET PRICES CHANGE

COMPETITION

Sellers decide what price things are sold at, and buyers decide whether or not to buy them from the supply available.

Imagine you have a stall at the apple market. To work out what price to sell your apples for, you would first look at what the other stallholders are selling them for.

↑ If you sell them at a higher price, people might decide to buy their apples at a cheaper stall and you won't sell many.

↓ But if you reduce the price a lot to try to sell more, you might end up with less profit margin and make a loss.

THE LAW OF SUPPLY AND DEMAND

SUPPLY

Companies decide how much to make at a particular price (taking into account production costs and profit margin).

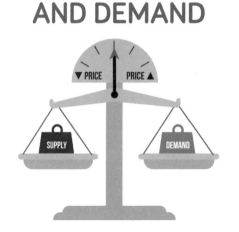

▼ PRICE   PRICE ▲

SUPPLY   DEMAND

DEMAND

Consumers decide how much to buy at a particular price (taking into account the options available on the market).

When supply and demand are the same, it is called MARKET EQUILIBRIUM.

When there are changes in supply or demand, the equilibrium price tends to change.

More supply than demand: When there is plenty of a product, or it is no longer popular, prices tend to go down. **↓**

More demand than supply: When there are shortages or when something suddenly becomes popular, prices tend to go up. **↑**

COMPETITION AND MONOPOLIES

Perfect Competition

Imagine you're at a farmer's market and you want to buy an apple. One farmer is selling her apples for $0.50, and another is selling his for $0.60. If the apples are the same size and neither is bruised or has a worm in it, then you would buy the cheaper apple. The other farmer would have to lower his price, otherwise no one would buy his apples. This is called **PERFECT COMPETITION**, where sellers offer identical products and they charge the same price as each other.

Imperfect Competition

However, perfect competition is very rare in real life. One farmer at the market may decide to sell a different type of apple, and if people prefer its flavor, they may be happy to pay a bit more for it. Or a person might decide to buy more expensive apples from a store that is closer to where they live, because it's quicker for them to go there than all the way to the market. This is **IMPERFECT COMPETITION**, where the products might be different, or there are few sellers.

Advertising and Brands

When companies are selling very similar products, they will use advertising to try to persuade people to buy their product rather than someone else's. A fast-food chain may say their burgers are made with healthier ingredients, or a company selling running shoes may say theirs are more comfortable or provide better grip.

Monopolies

When a single company controls the market, it doesn't have to worry about competition and is said to have a **MONOPOLY**. As it controls supply, it can decide how much of its product to put on the market and how much to charge for it. To stop companies being able to charge lots of money because people can't buy the product from anyone else, many countries have anti-monopoly laws.

SPECULATION

Speculation is a buying-and-selling operation with one aim: to **make money through reselling**. A speculator does not need the thing they buy. They just anticipate that the product will go up in price without needing to improve it, and they will **make a big profit from reselling it**.

In the market, there are big companies and investment funds that can put a lot of money into a market. These **massive investments** often cause **prices to go up** and mean that ordinary users and consumers cannot afford the inflated prices.

Property speculation

Some investment funds buy huge collections of property (houses, apartments, and other buildings) from banks, companies, and even governments.

This plays a part in rising demand and rising property prices in a particular area. As a result, many people can no longer afford housing and have to go and live somewhere else.

CAPITALISM

A capitalist is a person who has or can raise money (**CAPITAL**) to invest in a business. For example, they can build a factory and buy machinery.

The capitalist is the factory owner.

Some of the revenue will go toward buying more raw materials, paying the workers' wages, recovering the money spent to set up the factory, and buying better machinery. The rest of the money will go to the capitalist as profits.

The men and women who work in the factory transform raw materials into manufactured products. In exchange for this work, they are paid a salary.

These products are transported to markets and stores to be sold.

SHELBY & Co

The PROFITS that the capitalist makes will depend on the COSTS (such as the price of raw materials and the salary paid to the workers) and the REVENUE.

PROFIT = REVENUE – COSTS

The capitalist gets REVENUE from the sale of the products.

SALARIES

INCOME AND EXPENSES

  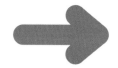

For most working people, a salary is the main source of income. But people can also receive income from investments (see page 36).

People and families have lots of expenses—the money they spend in their daily lives. Some expenses are regular, like food, rent, clothes, electricity, and water.

Others are one-off expenses that happen only rarely, such as buying a car or a house, or going on a vacation.

In exchange for the work they do, people earn money, a salary. There are lots of different kinds of work and jobs, whether it is working for a company, for a private individual, or for the state.

SAVINGS AND DEBT

Many people put aside some money as savings so they can pay for extra expenses. But there are also people whose salaries are so low that their regular expenses don't leave them enough money to be able to save.

When someone has no savings, or not enough, one option is to use debt. For example, buying a house is very expensive. Saving up to buy one could take years, so instead people can go to the bank and ask for a mortgage. That way they can have a house, but they stay in debt for many years (see page 21).

COUNTRIES

Humans have divided the planet into political units called countries. Each country is a distinct society that has symbols (such as a flag or a national anthem), a system of government, and its own laws.

Countries are also distinct economic units, which decide on economic policy. They have a central bank and they print their own money.*

Primary sector
The part of the economy that transforms natural resources into raw materials. It includes farming, mining, and livestock breeding.

Secondary sector
The factories and industries that transform raw materials into products to sell.

Tertiary sector
The services that are provided to businesses, industries, and consumers, such as transport, education, and banks.

Natural resources
Resources from nature used by humans, such as water, gas, and fish. They are finite and exploiting them can harm the environment.

Services and infrastructure
Transport networks, energy, clean water and wastewater systems, telecommunications, schools, hospitals, ports, and airports, as well as the services needed for the state to function, such as tax collection, police departments, offices, government ministries, and more.

* Countries such as France, Spain, and Germany are part of the European Union. That's why they share the same currency. They are a single market and most of their economic policy is decided by the Union's government and the European Central Bank.

The state needs money for lots of things, including building and maintaining schools, hospitals, and infrastructure (things like roads, railways, and sewers), and paying salaries to the police, the fire service, and soldiers. States collect **TAXES** from people and companies that live or operate in the country to pay for these things.

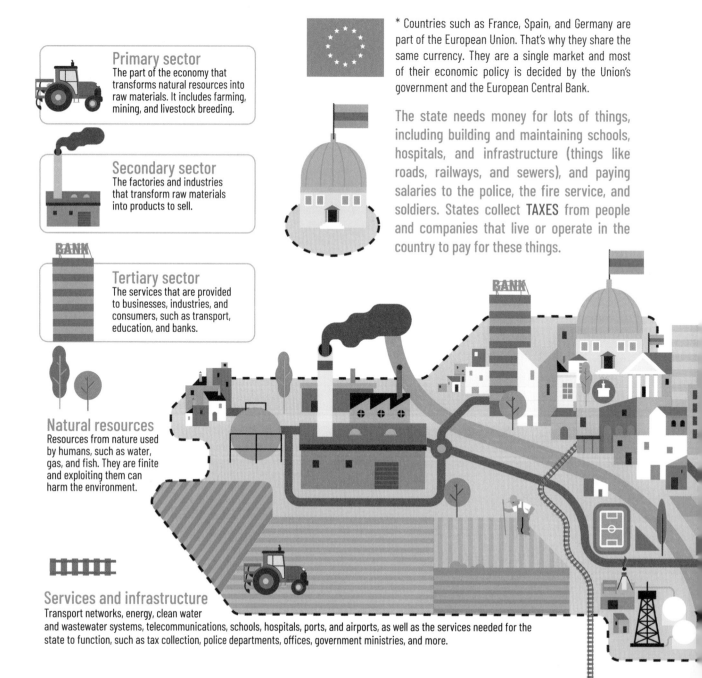

GDP

Like people, there are some countries that are richer and others that are poorer. One of the usual ways to work out a country's wealth is GDP (Gross Domestic Product).

GDP does not tell us about something that's very important: how fairly money is split between the rich and poor. A country can have a very high GDP, but most of the money might be owned by a small number of people, while people in the rest of the country are poor.

GDP is normally the total amount of money everyone in a country has produced in a year.

In other words, it is the value of everything made or used in a country over a year. This includes what we buy (cakes, haircuts, vacations, and so on), what companies invest in (for example, buying machinery), what our government spends money on (such as building roads), and how much we buy from and sell to other countries.

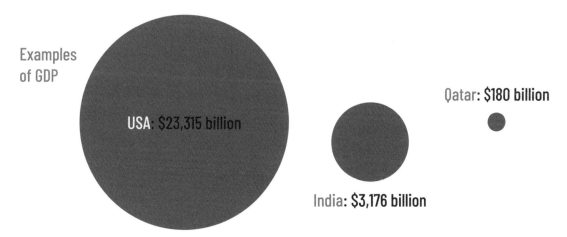

Examples of GDP

USA: $23,315 billion

India: $3,176 billion

Qatar: $180 billion

Source: data.worldbank.org

GDP PER CAPITA: this is GDP divided by the number of people in a country.

A country can have a very high GDP, but its wealth might be shared among lots of people or not many people (and remember that it might be shared out unequally, too).

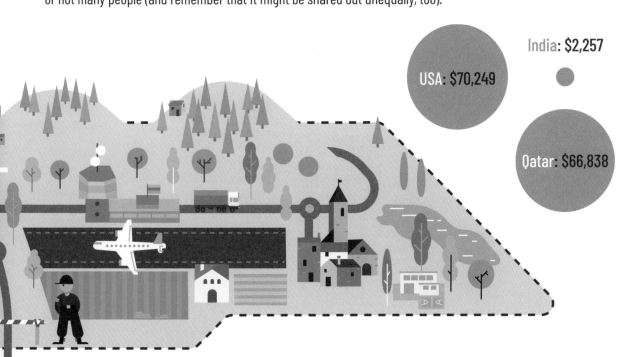

USA: $70,249

India: $2,257

Qatar: $66,838

Source: data.worldbank.org

THE ROLE OF THE STATE

After the Middle Ages, the idea of the modern state as we understand it today began emerging: it has a central government, the same laws for all its regions, a national economy, and taxes that individuals and companies have to pay.

But exactly what role should states play in the economy? Should people pay a lot of tax or not much? Not everyone sees it the same way.

Historically, the **classical** and **liberal** point of view is that **the state should intervene a minimal amount in the economy**. The role of the government is to make sure the market operates properly through laws, regulation, and security (such as police and the army).

Individuals and companies should be **free to compete and do business** while paying only **minimal taxes**. This will create wealth that will end up benefiting society as a whole.

The struggle between the two political and economic models caused a lot of political disputes, revolutions, coups d'état, and wars in the 19th and 20th centuries.

After the Second World War, the majority of European democracies opted for a model halfway between the two. On the one hand, they intervene in the economy to regulate prices, collect taxes, and make sure the economic and political system is stable.

However, the **communist** point of view sees things differently. It believes that there is a struggle between the dominant class (the rich) and the dominated class (the poor). Companies generate wealth only for the dominant classes by **exploiting workers** who have few labor, social, or political rights. For this reason, the means of production (factories) should be **owned by everyone**, and the state should **share out wealth** and guarantee rights and **equality** for everyone.

On the other hand, the state guarantees citizens' rights and responsibilities: people have to pay taxes and obey laws, but they also have rights like access to state education, social aid, medical care, and labor rights (such as the right to strike and to earn a minimum wage). This is a way to make sure society stays peaceful and to avoid conflict caused by big inequalities.

MULTINATIONALS

Thanks to the internet and modern transport methods, big companies and corporations can manufacture, sell, and move their money around the world.

EXAMPLES

Apple This brand of technology products has its headquarters in California (USA), but it manufactures mostly in China and has a network of its own stores all over the world.

Volkswagen Group This car manufacturer was originally a German company, but is now a multinational company that includes brands such as Audi, Škoda, Lamborghini, and SEAT.

Amazon This was one of the first online stores and it now has offices and warehouses in many countries.

Saudi Aramco Unlike the others, this Saudi Arabian company is state-owned. Although the oil it sells is extracted in its country, it has operations around the globe.

DELOCALIZATION

Companies want to make the maximum profit possible, and the most profitable way of manufacturing is to move production (or parts of it) to places where it will cost less: countries where taxes are low, wages are low, transport networks are efficient, and there are plenty of raw materials nearby.

So, for decades, many European and American companies have manufactured most of their products in countries such as China, Bangladesh, Mexico, and Morocco.

MARITIME TRANSPORT ROUTES

FINANCIAL CENTERS

Suez Canal

OIL AND GAS PIPELINES

Global GDP is now seven times higher than it was in the mid-20th century!

RAW MATERIALS

LAND TRANSPORT ROUTES

Source: https://data.worldbank.org/indicator/IS.SHP.GOOD.TU?

AND GLOBALIZATION

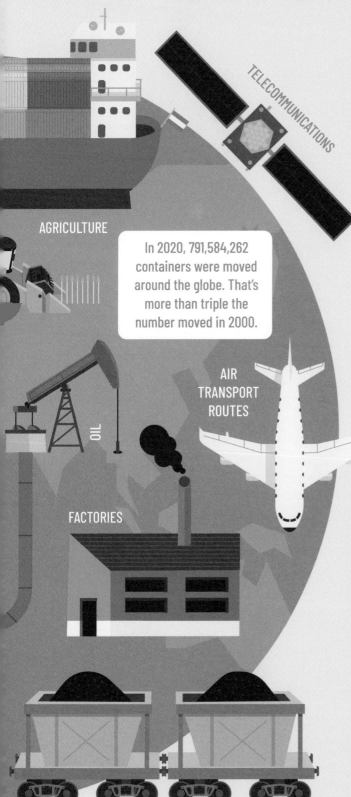

TELECOMMUNICATIONS

AGRICULTURE

> In 2020, 791,584,262 containers were moved around the globe. That's more than triple the number moved in 2000.

OIL

AIR TRANSPORT ROUTES

FACTORIES

RAIL TRANSPORT ROUTES

There are a number of organizations that make regulations for international trade, such as the **World Trade Organization**. Companies and countries (especially the richest ones) agree to follow these rules.

DUTIES AND TAXES

 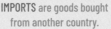 

IMPORTS are goods bought from another country.

EXPORTS are goods sold to another country,.

Countries charge taxes or limit the amount of goods that can enter or leave their territory. But there are areas such as the European Union that are "free trade zones," where goods can move between countries without any taxes being paid.

TAX HAVENS

There are countries that have more taxes than others. Some small countries and territories have specialized in having extremely low taxes and very little control over financial activities. These are known as tax havens.

Some companies and very rich people deposit money in the banks of these countries to avoid paying taxes in the countries where they live or work.

When the bank lends money, this doesn't just produce interest. As we will see, there are many ways for money to grow over time: this is called

INVESTING

Investing means putting money and effort into something that will give you returns in the future.

For example, a business person can invest in a machine to produce more.

Imagine a man who bottles water. He does it by hand and he can produce 100 bottles a week.

Then he sells them in a weekly market for $2 each. He earns $200 a week.

$2

But one day, he decides to invest in a machine that can produce 500 bottles of water a week. The machine costs $3,000. He only has $1,000 in savings, so he asks the bank to loan him $2,000.

$2

When he goes to the market, he sells all 500 bottles and he makes $1,000 a week.

Assuming that this man has no expenses, he doesn't have to pay interest on the loan, and he can save everything he's earned, after two weeks he can pay back the $2,000 that he borrowed from the bank to buy the machine.

And after one more week, he gets his $1,000 savings back too. He's got back what he invested, and he has the machine to be able to carry on making money.

INVESTMENTS

There are also lots of people and companies that invest in financial products that pay them interest. The more money you have, the more opportunity you have to try different products to make more profit.

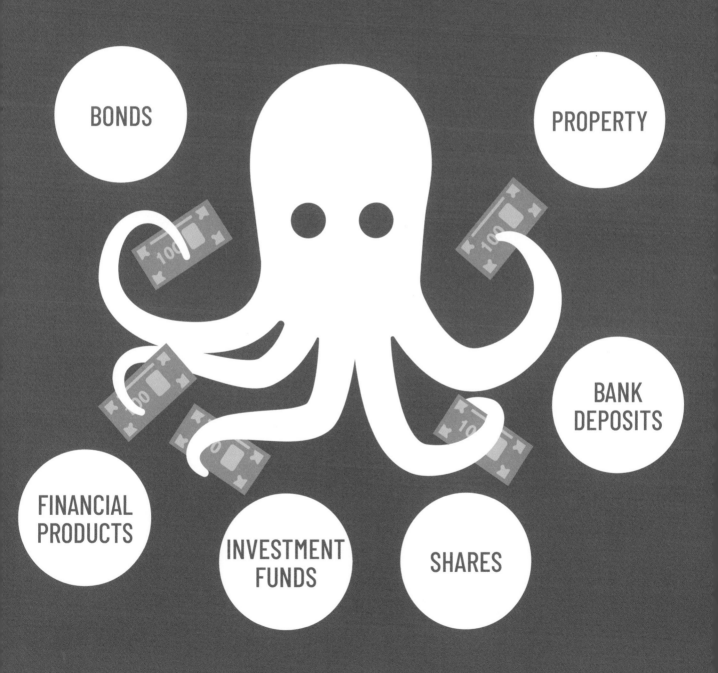

BONDS

PROPERTY

BANK DEPOSITS

FINANCIAL PRODUCTS

INVESTMENT FUNDS

SHARES

SHARES

Earlier on, you met the capitalist, the person who had enough money (capital) to own the factory. But many companies are not owned by just one person. Instead, they have several owners, who have different numbers of shares depending on how much money they invested.

These are the partners in a LIMITED COMPANY, a company with several different owners (partners).

Normally, partners in a limited company can only sell their shares to other partners or family members.
If they want to sell them to someone outside the company, they have to ask permission from the other partners.

Sometimes business people need lots and lots of money to create a new company
or to grow a limited company that already exists. In this case, they can do three things:

ASK THE BANK FOR MONEY
They'll have to pay back the money with interest after a period of time.

Ask for money

ISSUE BONDS
This means borrowing from investors (people or companies), rather than banks (see page 40).

ISSUE SHARES
Sell shares in the company to raise money. But to do this they need to become a **PUBLIC COMPANY**.

PUBLIC COMPANIES or PUBLIC LIMITED COMPANIES
are big companies whose capital is divided into shares held by many shareholders.

Imagine a limited company called AMAZE that needs money to carry on growing and making new investments. So it decides to float on the stock market, in other words become a public company and sell shares to raise money.

Public companies are very big companies.

So it calculates its share capital. This means it decides what the company is worth (the sum of what it owns, the money it has, the money it owes, the money it is owed, and so on). In this case, AMAZE calculates that its share capital is $100,000.

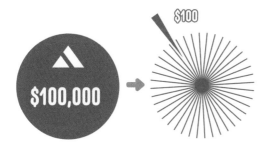

Next, it divides this capital between the shares that it wants to put on the market. If the company is worth $100,000 and it wants to issue a thousand shares, each share will be worth $100.

STOCK MARKET

The investors who buy these shares can be individuals or other companies. Buying shares in this way, directly from the company, is called the **PRIMARY MARKET***.

Normally, the company's profits are divided among the shareholders each year. The more shares a shareholder owns, the more profit they make.

A **board of directors** manages the company. Every year, it holds an **AGM** (a meeting of shareholders) to explain how the business is doing and what the profits will be. Shareholders can vote to change the board if they don't like what they're doing.

AMAZE

The vote of shareholders with lots of shares has more influence than the vote of shareholders with a few shares. So, if a company or individual owns more than half the shares, they control the decisions of the board of directors.

* People who own shares can then sell them to other people on the SECONDARY MARKET (see page 45).

BONDS

Apart from asking for loans from the bank, another way that companies and countries can raise money is by issuing BONDS.

Bonds are a way for investors to lend money for a period of time in exchange for interest (more or less like when the bank lends money).

Back in the 15th century, countries and cities that needed money to maintain armies and wage wars issued "public debt," in other words, they asked their citizens to lend them money in exchange for interest.

Today, countries still issue bonds, either at the national or regional level, to finance themselves. Along with taxes, this is the usual way that governments get the money they need to function.

As with any loan, the bonds state the amount borrowed, the time period, and the interest to be paid.

VALUE OF A BOND — $1,000 | $1,000 | 5 YEARS | 2%

For example, if we have a five-year bond of $1,000 with an annual interest rate of 2%, it means that for each bond we buy, we will make a profit of $20 every year and, when we get to the fifth year, we will be given our fifth $20 interest payment, plus the $1,000 initial investment. So, overall, we will have made a profit of $100.

1st year	2nd year	3rd year	4th year	5th year
+$20	+$20	+$20	+$20	+$20

$1,000 ⟶ $1,100 (+$100)

People who have bonds can sell them to other people on the SECONDARY MARKET (see page 45).

OTHER INVESTMENTS

Investors can invest their money in many other products, either to make interest or to speculate on the market. Here are some of the options:

PROPERTY INVESTMENT

Buying buildings, apartments, or houses. These can either be used (for example, for renting or setting up a business) or the investor can wait for the price to go up before selling them to make money.

INVESTING IN ART

There are people who buy art not because they like it, but because they expect the artist's works to become more popular in the future. In this way, the investors can resell the artworks at a higher price than they bought them.

PENSION FUNDS

These are investments that people make over the long term so that they have money for their retirement. The company that handles the pension fund uses this money to invest.

CURRENCY

You can buy currencies (such as dollars) when they are cheap in comparison to the currency you are using to buy them. Then, when the price goes up, you can sell them.

BUYING GOLD

Gold is what is called a "safe haven." It always has a high price and so is like a piggy bank, especially when the market is unstable and the value of money might vary.

STARTUPS

This involves investing in a company or project that is just starting up and needs money to grow. Entrepreneurs receive cash or advice from investors in exchange for shares or profits from the company.

INVESTMENT FUNDS

These are group investments that use money from lots of investors. They can invest in any of the investments we have mentioned, but they usually specialize in one thing (for example, shares).

CRYPTOCURRENCY

Like all things that vary in value, you can invest in cryptocurrency in the same way as currency: buy it when it is cheap and sell it when it is expensive.

THE STOCK EXCHANGE 1

Stock exchanges are places where people buy and sell shares, bonds, and other financial assets. There are stock exchange buildings in many cities around the world, but these days you can buy and sell equities from anywhere.

Before stock exchanges, there were commodity exchanges, which first appeared in Europe in the 12th century. Goods were bought and sold here, while loans and bonds were discussed in coffee houses, on streets, and in markets.

Stock exchanges as we understand them started in 1602 with the creation of the Dutch East India Company. Over 1,000 people invested their money in the company to fund trading trips to Asia, in return for a share of the profits from these trips. The shares in the company were called <u>stocks</u>, and they could be sold to other people at the offices of the company.

INTERMEDIARIES

<u>Brokers</u> are people authorized to act as intermediaries (go-betweens) between buyers and sellers of shares. Up until the late 1980s, it was normal to see them on the stock exchange floor (the place where they worked) shouting and making secret signs among themselves so that other brokers didn't know what they wanted to buy or sell.

Since the 1990s, this work has been done online and is available 24 hours a day (it is always open). Now anyone can buy or sell shares at any time from any computer. However, the majority of investors still use intermediaries, because it is very difficult to understand and follow the stock market.

BUYING AND SELLING SHARES

Earlier we looked at the primary market, when a company divides up its capital into shares and sells them on the stock exchange (page 39).

Now we're going to talk about the **secondary market**. If someone needs liquidity (cash to be able to buy or invest), they can sell the shares they have bought. Or, another time, they might decide to invest money by buying shares from someone who wants to sell them.

The price that shares are bought and sold for on the secondary market isn't the same price that the company who issued the shares sold them for. Instead, it **depends on supply and demand**:

Imagine we have two companies: AMAZE and TCKR

Both are big companies. They make phones and are listed on the stock market. But AMAZE makes stylish phones and is starting to become very famous, whereas TCKR is beginning to be a bit out-of-date, sells less than it used to, and has closed down some of its stores.

Investors want to own shares in the company that makes the most profit. So most of them want to buy AMAZE shares and not many want to buy TCKR shares. Therefore, as there is demand, AMAZE's shares will go up in price while TCKR's shares will go down.

AMAZE ▲ $110 (+10%)   TCKR ▼ $90 (-10%)

Both companies issued their shares at a price of $100 per share, but now AMAZE's shares are selling at $110, while TCKR's shares are worth just $90.

STOCK MARKET PANIC

When investors who have TCKR shares find out that the price is falling, some will want to sell their shares before the price falls even more. This causes the price to fall further, and so more investors sell their shares, and the price falls even more. So the shares lose more and more value in a "snowball" effect.

THE STOCK EXCHANGE ²

INFORMATION

To decide which equity they should invest in to make a profit, investors and brokers need lots and lots of information, such as if there is conflict in a country or if a company has made a bad investment and so might have financial problems.

With the arrival of the internet in the late 20th century, information began to circulate much faster, and nowadays you can buy and sell equities online from anywhere.

"PLAYING" THE STOCK MARKET

You can invest money in the stock market to buy many things: shares, bonds, commodities (see opposite page), and more. The idea behind this investment is that it generates a "return," or in other words, as time goes by, the money grows.

VOLATILITY

But there are also risks and unexpected events on the stock market: bankrupt companies, political decisions that affect the economy, fluctuations in currency markets that reduce profit margins, and more. This is called volatility, the danger of sudden fluctuations.

RISK

As a general rule, the riskier a stock market operation, the more profits you can make, but you can also lose a lot. Low-risk operations generate less profit, but it is harder to lose money.

STOCK INDEXES

A stock index is a number that is calculated from the share prices of a group of companies that represent a market (which can be anything from a country to a group of companies selling similar products or services). If an index goes up it's a sign of growth and optimism, and if it goes down it indicates a downturn and pessimism.

Some of the most important indexes are:

Dow Jones Industrial Average
Better known as Dow Jones. It is made up of 30 American companies.

Nasdaq 100
This is made up of 100 of the biggest non-financial companies on Nasdaq, an American stock exchange. Many are big tech companies such as Apple and eBay.

Euro Stoxx 50
This is the main European index. It includes the 50 leading companies in the Eurozone, including Volkswagen Group, Airbus, and Adidas.

Nikkei 225
This is the main Japanese index, made up of the 225 leading companies on the Tokyo Stock Exchange.

SSE Composite Index
This is the biggest index in China, made up of all the companies listed on the Shanghai Stock Exchange.

BONDS

There is also a secondary market in bonds that are bought and sold on stock exchanges.

For example, if we have bonds from a country but we know that this country has problems (like a war or an earthquake) that could put its economy at risk, investors try to get rid of these bonds because they're afraid they might not be paid the interest they're owed.

The more people who try to do this, the more the price will go down, and the more people will want to sell them, and the price will go down even more. However, some investors may think that the situation isn't that serious and take a risk by buying bonds very cheaply in the hope they'll go back up in value.

COMMODITIES

This is what we call staple products such as cereals (like wheat and soy), minerals (like copper, zinc, and iron), and even energy products like gas, oil, and coal.

These products are often bought on the so-called "futures market." For example, you can invest in next year's wheat harvest. In this way, intermediaries ensure a minimum price for farmers (they will earn money even if a storm affects the harvest), and if all goes well, buyers can resell the wheat at a higher price.

CRISIS AND RECESSION

GROWTH

One thing you will hear politicians talking about is GROWTH. They want the economy to grow year after year, but what actually happens is that there are cycles: sometimes the economy grows, sometimes it stagnates (doesn't change much), and sometimes it falls. When GDP goes down for two consecutive quarters (six months in total), it is called a RECESSION.

When this recession is very deep and goes on a long time, the economy is considered to be in CRISIS.

An ECONOMIC CRISIS can affect a region, a country or group of countries, or the whole world.

An economy is a very complicated system, with lots of interactions.

People work in factories, stores, and service companies

Products are sold by intermediaries

People buy things

THE SHOP

Products reach the markets

People buy houses

People buy houses

People pay taxes to the government

Banks lend money to governments

Banks lend money to people to buy houses

People work and deposit their money in the bank

Governments issue bonds, and their central bank lends money to banks

Banks lend money to companies that manufacture goods and provide services

%

%

%

%

%

%

Banks lend money to construction companies

Banks lend money to each other to generate interest

Banks invest in investment funds

%

LIKE A HOUSE OF CARDS

This whole chain of people, banks, institutions, and companies that buy, sell, consume, save, and lend money to each other is like a house of cards where each card supports the others.

But what happens if a natural disaster destroys the wheat harvest in a region or if a company goes bankrupt and can't pay back the money that the bank has loaned it?

Suddenly, the whole system can break, causing a chain reaction: investors are scared, there is panic on the stock market, banks don't lend money, many companies go bankrupt, lots of people end up with no job and no money and can't buy anything or pay the money they owe for their mortgage to the bank . . . The house of cards (or at least part of it) collapses and creates an ECONOMIC CRISIS. Then the house has to be built again . . .

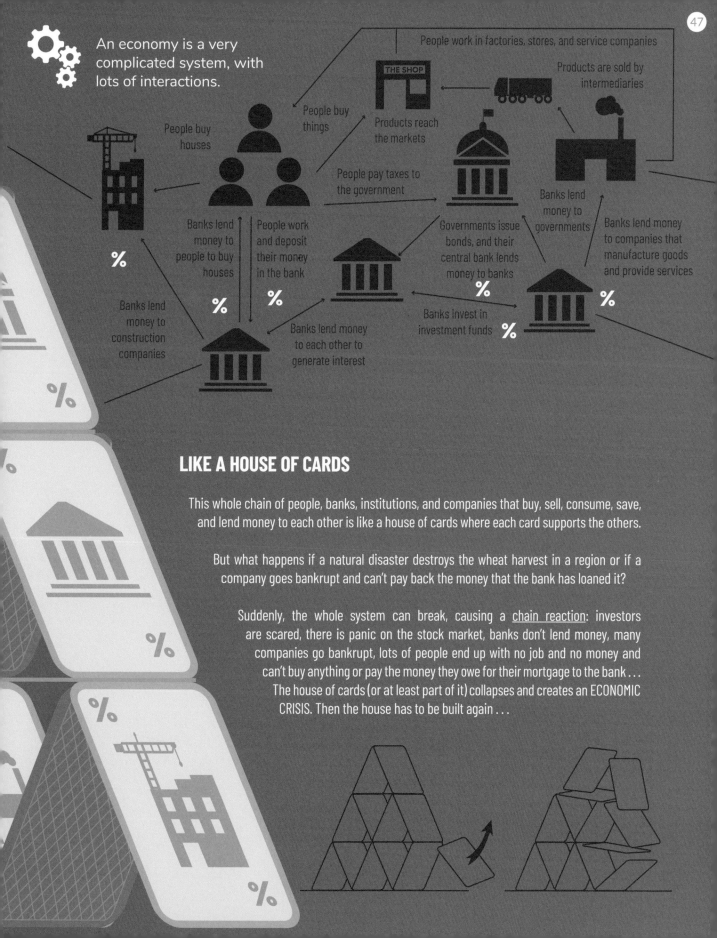

Throughout history there have been many economic crises that have been woven together with social, political, environmental, and other crises.

Sometimes the crises affect one country or region, but big crises have a global impact and they end up "infecting" all the world's economies.

Tulip bubble 1634

Panic of 1873

Stock market crash of 1929

1973 oil crisis

Black Monday 1987

2001 dot-com bubble

2008 financial crisis

1929 Crash and the Great Depression

This was one of the biggest crises that capitalism has ever had.

In 1929, in the United States, many people invested in the stock market. For various reasons, a stock market panic broke out and lots of people wanted to sell their shares.

I NEED A JOB

Very quickly, stocks fell by 70% and most shares lost their value, which ruined lots of companies and families that had invested in the stock market.

This financial crisis led to a deep economic and social crisis: the Great Depression. This made many economists think that capitalism without regulation is very dangerous for society.

THE TULIP BUBBLE

Tulips are very beautiful flowers. They came to Antwerp from Turkey in the 16th century and soon some varieties became a symbol of power and wealth for Dutch traders and the upper middle classes.

As there was a lot of demand, tulip bulbs became more and more expensive. There came a time when prices were going up so quickly that people were buying bulbs and selling them almost immediately at a higher price. Tulips were constantly changing hands

and more and more people got involved in buying and selling bulbs. The prices became astronomical: in an auction, a bulb could be worth as much as a house! People were even buying and selling bulbs that hadn't yet been planted.

But suddenly, some people sold their bulbs and didn't buy any more. Perhaps they were speculators who had already made enough money and understood that prices couldn't keep going up forever. People suddenly saw that the price of bulbs was silly, and

they tried to sell the ones they had. All of a sudden, there was a lot of supply and very little demand and prices fell dramatically: the "bubble" had burst, and many people who had invested fortunes in tulips were ruined.

POVERTY AND

Poor people are those who have access to a small amount of goods and services compared to everyone else in their society.

Extreme poverty
People in this situation are unable to meet their basic needs.

It is predicted that in 2030, 574 million people will still be living on less than $2.15 per day.

Source: www.worldbank.org/en/topic/poverty/overview

Public support
In rich countries, there are still many poor people, but governments spend money on education, public health, social services, and other systems to minimize extreme poverty.

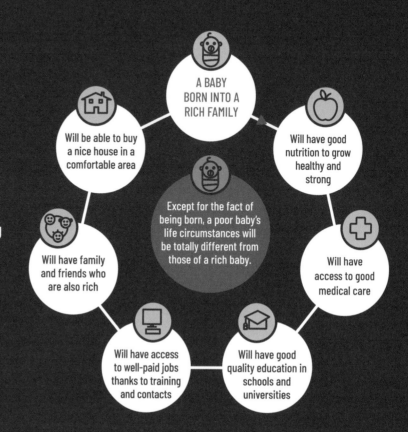

A BABY BORN INTO A RICH FAMILY

Will be able to buy a nice house in a comfortable area

Will have good nutrition to grow healthy and strong

Except for the fact of being born, a poor baby's life circumstances will be totally different from those of a rich baby.

Will have access to good medical care

Will have family and friends who are also rich

Will have good quality education in schools and universities

Will have access to well-paid jobs thanks to training and contacts

Many of the things we've learned about in this book aren't within the reach of poor people: partly because of their economic situation but also because of the education and the information they have. They cannot invest in the stock market, or buy property, or start a business, because the banks won't lend them money.

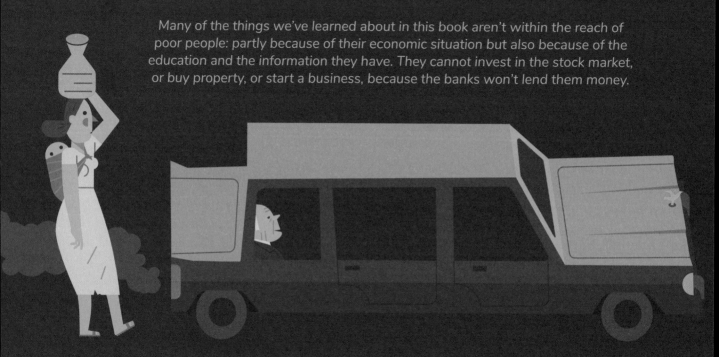

INEQUALITY

The resources available to us (such as oil, water, and raw materials) are limited. Economics studies how these resources are distributed.

 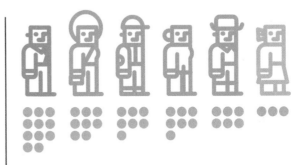

In a society where there is a big difference between a small group of very rich people and the vast majority of the population who live in poverty, we say that it is a society with many inequalities.

But if there is not much difference between the richest and the poorest, and wealth is distributed more evenly among the population, we say that it is a more egalitarian society.

It is natural that many economists, politicians, and thinkers wonder whether society should have an economy that favors equality and how to achieve this.

We start from an obvious principle: EVERYONE IS DIFFERENT AND HAS DIFFERENT CIRCUMSTANCES. We can be tall or short. We can be good at math or good at music (or both, or neither!). We can have rich or poor parents. We can be born in a country where everyone goes to school, or one where people find it hard to get jobs because of their gender, the color of their skin, or their religion.

ALL OF THESE CAN AFFECT YOUR ECONOMIC OPPORTUNITIES AND QUALITY OF LIFE.

RESPONSIBILITY

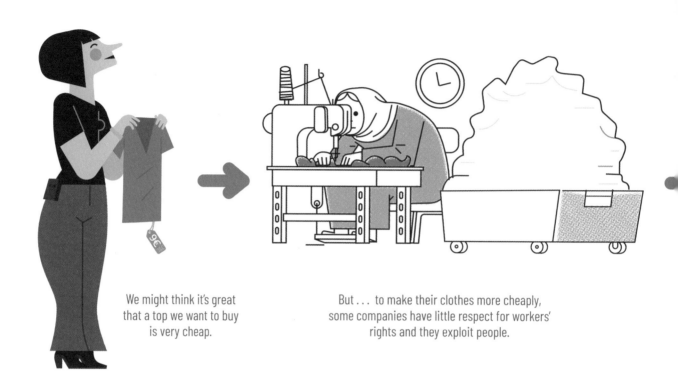

We might think it's great that a top we want to buy is very cheap.

But . . . to make their clothes more cheaply, some companies have little respect for workers' rights and they exploit people.

We are very happy because the money we have invested in an investment fund has made good profits.

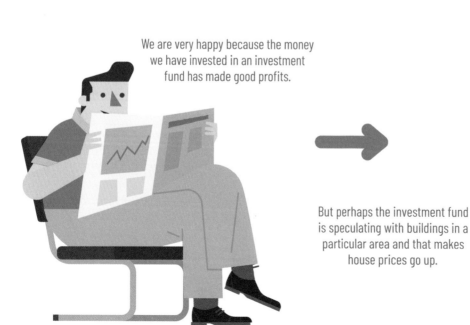

But perhaps the investment fund is speculating with buildings in a particular area and that makes house prices go up.

Companies aim to make profit, and this always has consequences, sometimes good and sometimes bad. When a pharmaceutical company discovers a drug, this can be good for society (it can cure people) and for the company (it can sell medicines). But on other occasions, a company doing business and making profit can have negative consequences for society.

Sometimes the cheapest way of doing things means the environment is polluted. Transporting products also causes a lot of pollution.

Then the price of rent goes up too, and lots of people who can't afford to pay it will have to leave the house where they live.

As consumers and customers, when we investing or spending our money we can choose companies that are responsible and understand that doing business should not have negative consequences for the planet.

GLOSSARY

asset
An item owned by a person or company that has an economic value.

bankrupt
A company or person who has run out of money and can't pay back what they owe to others.

barter
Exchanging goods or services to do business instead of using money.

bond
A loan for a set period of time that is repaid with interest at the end.

broker
A person who acts as an intermediary (go-between) between buyers and sellers of shares.

capitalism
An economic and political system where people can own land and property and buy and sell them to earn more capital (money). Someone who does so is a **capitalist**.

central bank
A special type of bank that decides how much money is available in the economy. This can affect the prices of the things we buy.

commodity
Basic objects, like wheat and oil, that are normally used by companies to make the products they sell.

communism
An economic and political system where land and property are owned by the government rather than individual people and wealth is shared.

competition
When two or more companies are selling the same thing and you can choose which one to buy from, they are in competition.

consumer
If you buy something and use it, rather than sell it to make a profit, you are a consumer.

cost
This is how much time, money, or work is needed to buy or make something.

cryptocurrency
A type of currency that only exists on computer networks and doesn't have any real coins or notes.

currency
The coins and notes, such as US dollars or British pounds, that people use to buy and sell things in a particular country.

debt
Money that is owed to someone else.

deflation
This means the cost of goods and services has gone down (the opposite of inflation).

demand
This is how many goods people want to buy at a certain price.

economics
The study of how resources, which are limited, are used by people and governments.

equity
The value of a company if it paid back any money it owed.

expenses
The money spent by a company or person.

globalization
Many companies operate in lots of countries all over the world, not just their home country. This allows them to make things more cheaply in other parts of the world where resources may cost less and wages may be lower, and it means they can sell their products to more people.

gold standard
An economic system where central banks can create coins and banknotes equal in value to how much gold they have. The value of coins and banknotes compared to gold doesn't change.

goods
These are useful items that can be bought and sold. Some goods are tangible (we can touch them), like a computer or a loaf of bread, while others are intangible (we can't touch them), like a song bought on an app.

gross domestic product (GDP)
This is the value of everything made or used in a country over a year.

inflation
This means the cost of goods and services has gone up (the opposite of deflation).

interest
When someone borrows money, the person they borrow the money from will ask for extra money to be paid back, which is called interest.

investing
This means putting money and effort into something that will give you more money in the future. People who do this are **investors**.

market equilibrium
This when the amount of goods or services at a particular price (the supply) is the same as how much of them people want to buy (the demand).

markets
Places where things are bought and sold.

money
This is something that people agree has a value and is used to buy and sell goods and services.

monopoly
When only a single company provides specific goods or services for the market, it is said to have a monopoly.

multinational
A company that is based in more than one country.

profit
A person's or a company's profit is the amount of money they have after they have sold what they make.

producer
This is someone who creates goods or provides services for others.

recession
A long period of time when people are producing and selling fewer things and more people are unemployed.

reserves
Money set aside by banks that they are not allowed to lend to anyone, so that if someone would like to take out some money from their bank account, then the bank has enough to give it to them.

resources
These are the things that are used to create goods and services. They can be stuff you can touch, such as water or oil, and they can also be people who create or provide the goods or services.

revenue
The money received when something is sold.

services
These are things that can be bought, but (unlike goods) are actions rather than objects. Scissors are goods, but having your hair cut by someone is a service, and cars are goods, but a taxi ride is a service.

shares
When a company's ownership is divided up between people, each part is called a share and the people who own them are called the **shareholders**.

speculation
This is buying something in order to make more money by reselling it at a higher price in the future.

stock exchange
Stock exchanges are places where people buy and sell shares, bonds, and other financial assets.

supply
This is how much of something there is for people to buy—when supply increases, it means people can buy more of it than before.

surplus
When there is more of an asset or resource available than people and companies need, the unwanted amount is called the surplus.

tax
Money that governments charge companies and people to pay for services like the police, and schools.

trading
Buying and selling goods is called trading. People who trade are called **traders**.

value
This is how much something is worth. It can change depending on personal tastes, and also circumstances—you may think an apple has low value if you don't like apples, but you may think it has more value if there is nothing else to eat.

wealth
This is the value of everything a person or company owns added up together.

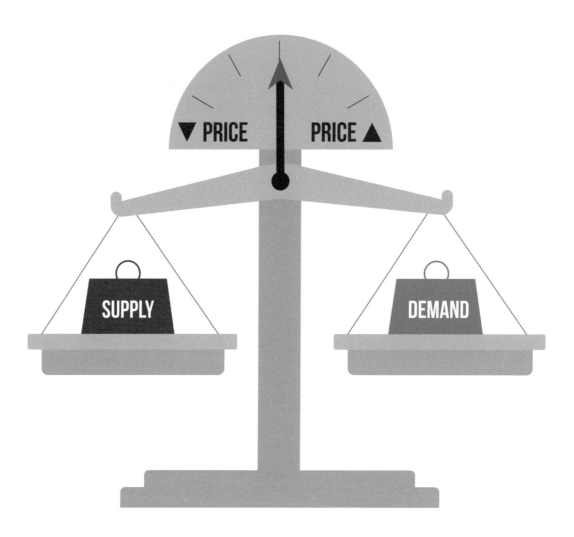

For Alababalà, Consultant: Marc Gallifa; Designer and Editor: Meli. For GMC Publications, Publisher: Jonathan Bailey; Production Director: Jim Bulley; Senior Project Editor: Tom Kitch; Design Manager: Robin Shields; English Translation: Andrea Reece; Editor: Claire Saunders; Publishing Assistant: Charlotte Mockridge; Editorial Advisors: Lucas Chari, Pawel Dziewulski, and Annemie Maertens. Color origination by GMC Reprographics. Printed and bound in China.